21st Century Junior Library

UNDERSTANDING WILDFIRES

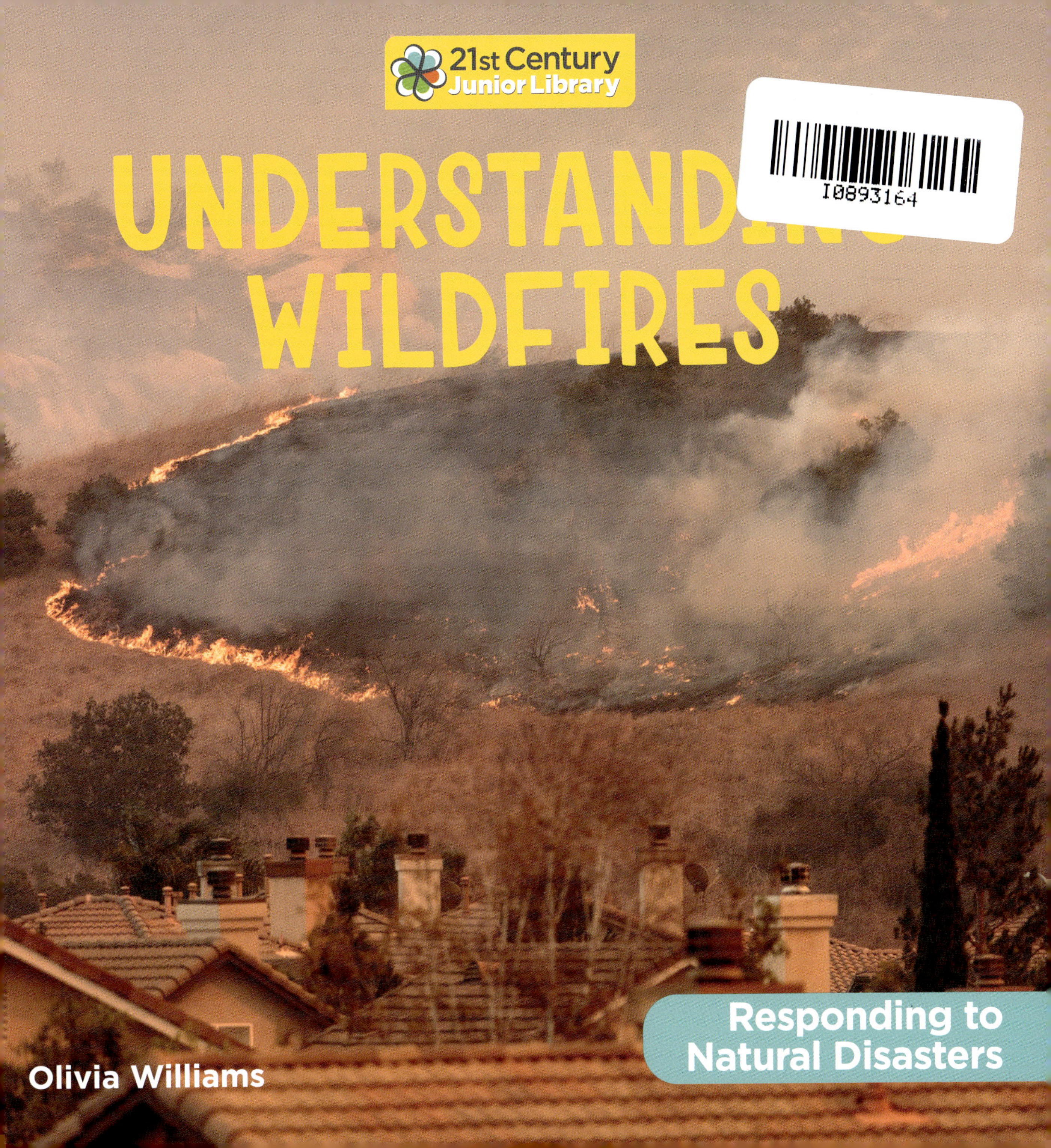

Responding to Natural Disasters

Olivia Williams

Published in the United States of America by:

CHERRY LAKE PRESS
2395 South Huron Parkway, Suite 200, Ann Arbor, Michigan 48104
www.cherrylakepress.com

Reading Adviser: Beth Walker Gambro, MS, Ed., Reading Consultant, Yorkville, IL
Photo Credits: © Aarti Kalyani/Shutterstock.com, cover, 1; U.S. Fish and Wildlife Service Headquarters/Flickr/Photo by Greg Sanders, USFWS; © trekandshoot/Shutterstock.com, 6; © Daria Nipot/Shutterstock.com, 7; © KeongDaGreat/Shutterstock.com, 9; © Flystock/Shutterstock.com, 10, 11; © /Shutterstock.com, 12; © heathercharise/Shutterstock.com, 13 [top, left]; © Africa Studio/Shutterstock.com, 13 [top, right]; © Trevor Bexon/Shutterstock.com, 13 [bottom, left]; © Roman Kosolapov/Shutterstock.com, 15 [top]; © NPS Photo, 15 [bottom]; © U.S. Department of Agriculture/flickr/Photo by Mike McMillan, 16; © Holden Law/Shutterstock.com, 19; © Bureau of Land Management Oregon and Washington/flickr/Photo by Cheyne Rossbach, 20 [right]

Cherry Lake Press is an imprint of Cherry Lake Publishing Group.

Library of Congress Cataloging-in-Publication Data
Names: Williams, Olivia (Writer of children's books), author.
Title: Understanding wildfires / Olivia Williams.
Description: Ann Arbor, MI : Cherry Lake Publishing, [2022] | Series: Responding to natural disasters | Audience: Grades 2-3
Identifiers: LCCN 2021043051 | ISBN 9781534199217 (hardcover) | ISBN 9781668900352 (paperback) | ISBN 9781668906118 (ebook) | ISBN 9781668901793 (pdf)
Subjects: LCSH: Wildfires—Juvenile literature.
Classification: LCC SD421.23 .W59 2022 | DDC 363.37/9—dc23
LC record available at https://lccn.loc.gov/2021043051

Cherry Lake Press would like to acknowledge the work of the Partnership for 21st Century Learning, a Network of Battelle for Kids. Please visit http://www.battelleforkids.org/networks/p21 for more information.

Printed in the United States of America
Corporate Graphics

ABOUT THE AUTHOR

Dr. Olivia Williams is from mid-Wales in the United Kingdom. She has traveled to many countries to help people after natural disasters. She has felt earthquakes and aftershocks, and seen damage from floods, typhoons, and wildfires. The natural environment can be harsh but also beautiful. Olivia loves to hike and run in the mountains and photograph the incredible things she sees.

CHERRY LAKE PRESS

CONTENTS

WHAT ARE WILDFIRES?

A wildfire is a large and uncontrollable fire. Wildfires occur in many ways. Wildfires can start when lightning or **lava** touches dry plants. Wildfires usually occur in the summer, when trees, grasses, and leaves are dry. This means they burn more easily. Wildfires are also created by the **decomposition** of vegetation. The vegetation becomes so hot that it suddenly creates a flame.

Some wildfires can produce fire whirls, or fire tornadoes.

Wildfires can be made worse by wind, heat, and **drought**. Scientists think climate change is partly to blame, as it makes Earth hotter. When the environment is hot, wildfires are more likely to occur.

Some communities are more **vulnerable** to wildfires than others.

The Black Friday Bushfire affected the surrounding soil so much that it took several decades for it to return to normal.

The biggest single wildfire occurred in 1939 in Australia. This fire is called the Black Friday Bushfire. It burned 4.9 million acres (2 million hectares) and killed 71 people. In 2020, western U.S. states experienced dangerous wildfires too. The wildfires created huge amounts of smoke.

The smoke crossed the United States and the Atlantic Ocean and reached Europe!

Wildfires are **natural disasters**. But not all wildfires are started by nature. Sometimes they are started by people. People can be careless when they are out in nature. Campfires and lit cigarettes can cause wildfires. Sun shining through glass can too. At other times, **arson** can be the cause.

Think!

Imagine you are walking in the woods with your friends. Suddenly, you see smoke coming from an old campfire. You know that it is dangerous to leave it burning. You are worried that a fire could harm the animals and vegetation around it. What do you think you and your friends should do?

Wildfires are a common occurrence in areas like Australia and California.

HOW WILDFIRES AFFECT THE PLANET AND PEOPLE

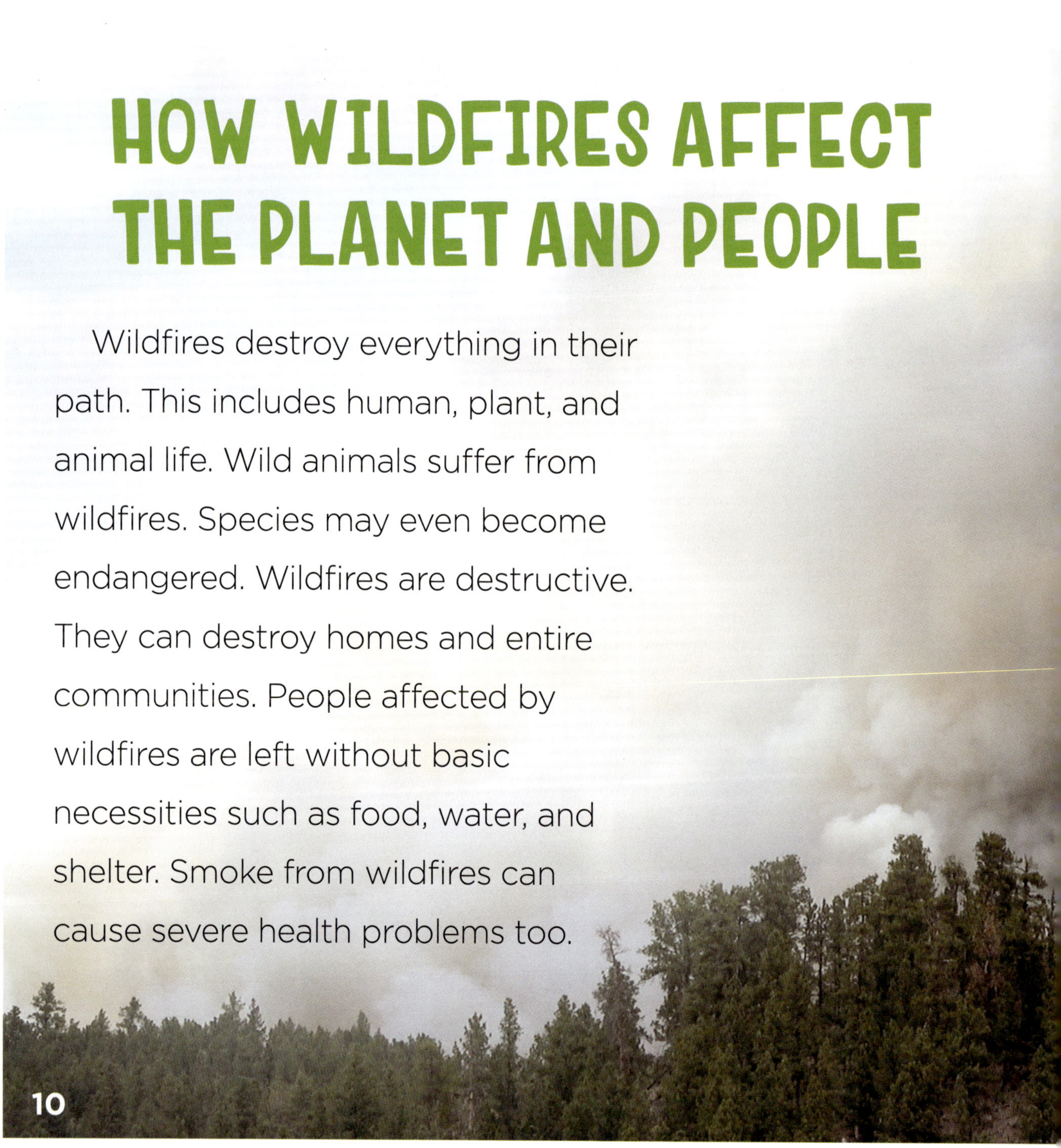

Wildfires destroy everything in their path. This includes human, plant, and animal life. Wild animals suffer from wildfires. Species may even become endangered. Wildfires are destructive. They can destroy homes and entire communities. People affected by wildfires are left without basic necessities such as food, water, and shelter. Smoke from wildfires can cause severe health problems too.

Wildfires are becoming more common. Even cold Arctic countries and regions like Russia and Siberia can have wildfires. In 2021, the smoke from wildfires in Russia could be seen from space! Scientists believe many landscapes they once called **fire-resistant** are actually **fire-prone**. They realized that carbon can burn under ice without a flame. Carbon-rich soil called peat burns at a low temperature without making flames. Smoke and **methane** are

Wildfires happen so often that people consider it a fifth season: spring, summer, fall, winter, and fire season.

then released when the ice melts. Scientists call this a **zombie fire**. Zombie fires further increase global warming and harm the planet.

Wildfires may be destructive, but sometimes they can have positive effects. Wildfires can help plants and living things. Giant sequoia trees rely on fires to help release seeds that produce more trees. **Indigenous peoples** know a lot about wildfires. They have reported that birds use wildfires as an opportunity to find food. They have seen

Ask Questions!

Wildfires are occurring in colder climates with ice and snow. People in those places are worried about wildfires affecting their traditions and way of life. Go online to find out which cultural traditions might be affected.

birds pick up hot vegetation and then drop it. This sets fire to the grass. Small animals are forced to move away from the fire. The birds see the moving animals and eat them.

Scientists studying the effects of wildfires have noticed an increase in wood-boring insects. Wood-boring insects eat burned and decomposing wood. Birds like quail and woodpeckers feed on these insects. In this way, wildfires can positively affect the food chain.

Interagency Hotshot Crews consist of firefighters who specialize in fighting wildfires.

PROTECTING AGAINST AND RECOVERING FROM WILDFIRES

People fight wildfires in several ways. Earth-moving diggers, dump trucks, and fire trucks with water hoses all help. Airplanes and helicopters spread water over wildfires from above. Firefighters also play an important role in fighting wildfires. They have a lot of experience controlling raging fires. **Satellites** and drones track the direction wildfires move. They also watch how big the fire becomes. This information helps firefighters plan how to attack the fire.

Some specialist firefighters parachute into wildfires in remote areas. These highly trained firefighters are called smokejumpers. Good forest management is also important. Using methods such as **firebreaks** help to stop the spread of wildfires.

The California Wildfire Relief Fund helps people after wildfires. It gives money and support to

Look!

Take a look around your community. Which neighbors are the most in need? What areas need the most protection? Write out a plan on how you think your community can come together to help! Then, ask a police officer or firefighter what they think of your plan.

Wildfires can negatively affect the quality of water in the surrounding area.

Communities can work together to build back what was lost.

people who need it. Money helps people to rebuild their homes, buy new furniture, and pay medical bills. Support helps people find new jobs and take care of their families.

Make a Guess!

Imagine you live in the countryside. There has been a wildfire in your community. Your neighbors' houses have been burned, and farmers have lost their crops. Your neighbors and local farmers are frightened and worried. What kind of things might they be worried about? Discuss your thoughts with a friend.

ACTIVITY

Create a Go-Bag

Go-bags are bags that contain important supplies you'll need during an evacuation. With a go-bag, you'll be even more prepared! Below is a list of a few essential items you may need. Can you think of anything else you'd add?

- Money
- Medicine
- First-aid kit
- Water
- Canned and dry food
- Clothes
- Hand sanitizer
- Flashlight
- Umbrella

GLOSSARY

arson **(AHR-suhn)** the illegal burning of a building or other property

decomposition **(dee-kahm-puh-ZIH-shuhn)** the process of dead organic matter rotting or decaying

drought **(DROWT)** a long period of little to no rain

firebreaks **(FYR-brayks)** gaps in an area that act as a barrier to slow or stop wildfires from spreading

fire-prone **(FYR-PROHN)** easily catches fire

fire-resistant **(FYR-ri-ZIH-stuhnt)** does not easily catch fire

Indigenous peoples **(in-DIH-juh-nuhss PEE-puhls)** peoples who were the first to live in an area or region

lava **(LAH-vuh)** hot liquid rock that exists above the ground

methane **(MEH-thayn)** a colorless, odorless gas that burns easily

natural disasters **(NAH-chuh-ruhl dih-ZAH-stuhrz)** natural events such as a floods, earthquakes, or hurricanes that cause great damage

satellites **(SAT-uhl-ahytz)** machines sent into space that move around the Earth

vulnerable **(VUHL-nuh-ruh-buhl)** capable of being easily hurt or injured, like small children, the elderly, or animals

zombie fire **(ZAHM-bee FYR)** underground fire fueled by methane deposits and covered by a layer of snow or ice; zombie fires can burn through cold and wet Arctic winters

FIND OUT MORE

Book

Thiessen, Mark. *Extreme Wildfire: Smoke Jumpers, High-Tech Gear, Survival Tactics, and the Extraordinary Science of Fire.* Washington, D.C.: National Geographic Kids, 2016.

Websites

Preventing Wildfires

https://smokeybear.com/en/smokey-for-kids/preventing-wildfires
Visit Smokey Bear to learn more about preventing wildfires.

Smokejumpers—These Firefighters Parachute Directly into Wildfires

https://www.youtube.com/watch?v=_Cawz3HsJL0
Learn about these heroic men and women.

Why the Giant Sequoia Needs Fire to Grow

https://youtu.be/lmNZGr9Udx8
Watch and learn how fire can help the Giant Sequoias.

INDEX